RECLAIMING CONSTITUTIONAL AUTHORITY THROUGH THE 'POWER OF THE PURSE'

CONTENTS

Abstract ………………………………………………………………………………..	Page iii
Budgeting and Governing……………………………………………………………	Page 1
Constitutional Authority for the 'Power of the Purse'……………………………….	Page 2
How Current Budget Practices Undermine Congress's Authority……………………..	Page 3
Restoring Constitutional Government……………………………………………..	Page 8
Conclusion………………………………………………………………………...	Page 11
Contributors……………………………………………………………………….	Page 13

ABSTRACT

Choosing priorities and allocating financial resources is the most straight-forward way for a legislature to shape governing policies. Moreover, a government's budgeting system is central to determining the kind of governing system a country has. Hence, a vigorous practice of budgeting is fundamental to Congress's policymaking authority under Article I of the Constitution.

The United States' Federal Government is not a parliamentary system. To the extent Congress cedes control of the budget, the Executive Branch – which is independent of Congress – gains power, undermining the Constitution's carefully drawn balance of powers. The Founders established this constitutional system precisely to prevent such concentrations of power, which would ultimately threaten individual freedoms. Therefore, the budget process must strive to reinforce Congress's constitutional authority and the U.S. Government's arrangement of three separate but coequal branches.

BUDGETING AND GOVERNING

Earlier this year, Judge Rosemary M. Collyer of the United States District Court in Washington, DC issued a ruling that reasserted the power of the purse as one of Congress's most important instruments for governing. Judge Collyer ruled the Obama Administration had violated the Constitution by reimbursing health insurers for discounts on copays and deductibles under the Affordable Care Act [ACA]. Congress had expressly refused to appropriate funds for that purpose, so the administration drew resources from other accounts in the health care program. In rejecting the administration's actions, Judge Collyer's ruling said in part: "Congress is the only source for such an appropriation, and no public money can be spent without one."[1]

Following the decision, *The Wall Street Journal* editorial page opined: "The ruling is a vindication of the separation of powers under the Constitution, which in Article I gives Congress sole power over spending. This is a crucial check on tyranny. If a President can combine the legislative power to spend with the power to execute laws, he can ignore Congress and govern by whim."[2]

Judge Collyer put implementation of the decision on hold so the administration could appeal. Nevertheless, if her ruling ultimately is upheld, it could undermine the ACA by defunding this provision. Insurers might find it too expensive to absorb the costs and either hike up premiums or leave the ACA's exchanges altogether, reducing competition. Thus, a simple, fundamental act of budgeting – Congress's decision not to appropriate funds for a particular purpose – would have a direct effect on policy, by reasserting one of Congress's most important governing authorities: control over spending.

This is just one specific example showing how the power of the purse truly is essential to Congress's governing authority, and consequently to the entire constitutional system. If Congress does not exercise its control over spending and taxing, it fails to govern and threatens the dynamic equilibrium of the balance of powers. As James Madison famously wrote: "This power of the purse may, in fact, be regarded as the most complete and effectual weapon with which any constitution can arm the immediate representatives of the people, for obtaining a redress of every grievance, and for carrying into effect every just and salutary measure."[3]

Most discussions of budget process reform focus on the practical mechanisms of budgeting, and evaluate the budget's constitutional role only secondarily, if at all. In truth, however, the budget is a principal means of policymaking and of exercising constitutional government. "[T]he budget is much more than a matter of dollars. It finances federal programs and agencies and is a vital means of establishing and pursuing national priorities. In a fundamental sense, the federal government is what it spends."[4]

---

[1] *United States House of Representatives v. Burwell et al*, Civil Action No. 14-1967 (D.D.C. 12 May 2016), p. 13.
[2] "Vindicating Congress's Power of the Purse," *The Wall Street Journal*, 12 May 2016: http://www.wsj.com/articles/vindicating-congresss-power-of-the-purse-1463094840.
[3] *The Federalist*, No. 58.
[4] Allen Schick, *The Federal Budget: Politics, Policy, Process* – Third Edition (Washington, DC: Brookings Institution Press, 2007), p. 14.

To put it another way: "The budget in practically all current discussions is treated as an incidental or a minor thing. It is regarded primarily as a matter of finance or of accounting procedure. It is viewed too often merely as a question of the manipulation of figures. While as a matter of fact instead of being a secondary thing it is of the first importance; instead of being a subordinate thing it is a fundamental thing; instead of being merely the manipulation of figures it is decisive in its relation to the health, education and welfare of all the citizens and residents of the state or nation concerned."[5]

CONSTITUTIONAL AUTHORITY FOR THE 'POWER OF THE PURSE'

Although America's Founders had little sense of formalized budget practices, they knew control over spending and taxation was one of the most powerful instruments of government – one that had to rest with the legislature. "Centuries of struggle in England between Parliament and the Crown over the power of the purse culminated in the principle that the government's authority to tax and spend must be conferred by legislation. It took centuries to implant this principle in England, but by the time the American colonies were waging war for their independence, its acceptance on this side of the Atlantic was a basic tenet of limited, democratic government."[6]

Indeed, budgeting plays a critical role in maintaining the constitutional order itself: "When you have decided on your budget procedure you have decided on the form of government you will have as a *matter of fact*. Make the executive the dominating and controlling factor in budget-making and you have, irrespective of what label you put on it, an autocratic actual government. If, recognizing the large part the executive or the administration may play in budget-making, you give the dominating and controlling influence to the representatives of the people elected to the legislature, you have, irrespective of what label you put on it, a democratic or a representative actual government."[7]

The most often-cited source of Congress's power of the purse is the constitutional requirement that Federal spending can occur only pursuant to an appropriations act (Article I, Section 9). In fact, however, the congressional budgeting authority lies in several provisions of the Constitution:

- Article I, Section 7, First Clause: "All Bills for raising revenue shall originate in the House of Representatives; but the Senate may propose or concur with Amendments as on other Bills."

- Article I, Section 8, First Clause: "The Congress shall have the Power To lay and collect Taxes, Duties, Imposts and Excises, to pay the Debts and provide for the common Defence and general Welfare of the United States; but all Duties, Imposts and Excises shall be uniform throughout the United States;"

- Article I, Section 8, Second Clause: [The Congress shall have the Power] "To borrow money on the credit of the United States;"

---

[5] Edward Augustus Fitzpatrick, *Budget Making in a Democracy* (New York: The MacMillan Company, 1918), p. vii.
[6] Schick, op. cit., p. 10.
[7] Fitzpatrick, op. cit., p. viii.

- Article I, Section 9, Seventh Clause: "No Money shall be drawn from the Treasury, but in Consequence of Appropriations made by Law; and a regular Statement and Account of the Receipts and Expenditures of all public Money shall be published from time to time."

- Amendment XVI: "The Congress shall have the power to lay and collect taxes on incomes, from whatever source derived without apportionment among the several States, and without regard to any census or enumeration."[8]

Notwithstanding this authority, the Constitution prescribes no particular budgeting procedures. Those came about from practices that started from the beginning of the republic and evolved over time, eventually leading to formal budget laws and rules in the House and Senate.[9] This tangle of laws and procedures has contributed to the complexity of today's budget process, making budgeting itself more difficult.

HOW CURRENT BUDGET PRACTICES UNDERMINE CONGRESS'S AUTHORITY

When adopted in 1974, the Congressional Budget Act sought to reassert legislative control over budgeting after several years of discord between Congress and the President. Nevertheless, as the process has evolved, various procedures, or failures in budget practices, have come to actually erode Congress's policymaking authority, sometimes ceding power, in concrete ways, to the Executive Branch. The following discussion presents some examples.

The President's Budget

Until the early 20th century, the Federal Government had no formal or comprehensive budgeting procedure. Generally, agency heads would visit their respective committees of jurisdiction on Capitol Hill and submit their budget requests, with no overall coordination by the White House, and the committees would determine how much to provide. This was a period of legislative dominance over budgeting.

"The various requests were compiled by the Treasury in an annual *Book of Estimates*, but little effort was made to coordinate spending by individual agencies or to ensure that they totaled to an acceptable amount and were in accord with national policy."[10] Congress controlled not only the totals, but also individual spending items by making detailed appropriations. Through this period, balancing budgets was the fiscal norm during peacetime. "Financial stability was maintained despite the lack of a presidential budget system to coordinate revenues and expenditures. As long as the government was small and its financial needs modest, a national budget was not necessary for producing acceptable outcomes."[11]

---

[8] See Committee on the Budget, U.S. House of Representatives, *A Compendium of Laws and Rules of the Congressional Budget Process*, Committee Print Serial No. CP-1, August 2015, pp. 580-582.
[9] Ibid.
[10] Schick, op. cit., p. 14.
[11] Ibid., p. 13.

The stability began to break down in the early 20th century. Between 1894 and 1915, Federal spending doubled in nominal terms, producing chronic deficits. "Spending exceeded revenues in 11 of the 17 years from 1894 to 1910."[12] World War I (then known as The Great War) caused spending to soar, from $726 million in 1914 to $19 billion five years later. "The public debt followed a similar trend in those five years, escalating from $1 billion to $26 billion."[13] That was about 33 percent of gross domestic product [GDP] at the time. (Today, the Federal Government's publicly held debt is 75.4 percent of GDP, and gross debt – including amounts owed to government accounts – is about 104 percent of GDP.[14])

Progressive reformers at the time – favoring "experts" over politicians – encouraged a more centralized, administrative form of government. They expressed this impulse, in part, by proposing an organized practice of Federal budgeting, situated in the Executive Branch. This led to adoption of the Budget and Accounting Act of 1921.[15] Briefly, the act contained the following main elements:

- It required the President to submit to Congress every year a comprehensive budget reflecting all the agencies' requests.

- It created the Bureau of the Budget (renamed the Office of Management and Budget in 1971), originally situated in the Treasury Department.

- It also created the General Accounting Office (now the Government Accountability Office) to provide congressional oversight of Executive Branch fiscal activities.

The arrangement was consciously modeled on that of the United Kingdom. "A simile – be like Britain – justified recommendations for budget hierarchy in the United States."[16] Thus, the Budget and Accounting Act imposed on the U.S. Constitution's arrangement of three separate but coequal branches of government a budget procedure designed for a parliamentary system.

The President's budget never had any legislative authority – it still does not – but it provided the President with a platform to spell out a national agenda. Although actual spending and taxation still could result only from acts of Congress, congressional action on fiscal matters was piecemeal. Only the President's budget reflected an overall view of the government. President Franklin D. Roosevelt understood the value of this instrument for shifting control of government and policy to the Executive Branch. "[T]he seeds of a new form of governing had been sown. The initial change can be seen in the New Deal, which brought significant new interventions in the national economy and the creation of the entitlement programs that threaten our fiscal stability today. FDR recognized the constitutional significance of this shift when he moved the Bureau of the Budget (established under the 1921 Budget and Accounting Act) from the Treasury to the new

---

[12] Ibid., p. 14.
[13] Ibid., p. 14.
[14] Congressional Budget Office, *Updated Budget Projections: 2016-2026*, March 2016.
[15] Public Law 67-13, 42 Stat. 20, enacted 10 June 1921.
[16] Aaron B. Wildavsky, *The New Politics of the Budgetary Process* – Third Edition (New York: Addison-Wesley Educational Publishers Inc., 1997), p. 35.

Executive Office of the President, establishing that henceforth control of the budget would be key to controlling and directing the new form of American government."[17]

After World War II, presidents consciously expanded the use of the budget to express their policy agendas. "During the 1950s and 1960s, it became customary for the president to prepare a legislative program in tandem with the annual budget. The president used the budget to propose spending initiatives, which shaped Congress's agenda and media coverage. . . . This was the age of the 'imperial presidency,' a term coined by scholars to characterize the extent to which the president dominated national policy. The budget was one of his chief tools, enabling him to formulate programs, promote spending initiatives, and preside over a new burst of governmental expansion that culminated in the Great Society legislation enacted in 1964 and 1965."[18]

Following several years of conflict between the White House and the legislature, lawmakers in 1974 adopted the Congressional Budget Act. It was intended to restore congressional power over budgeting, and at least theoretically, it did: Individual spending and tax bills would now be written pursuant to the congressional budget resolution – a new instrument created under the Budget Act – rather than the President's budget. "The budget resolution augmented the wholly decentralized approach that had existed to that point, in which individual committees considered pieces of the budget, but the Congress never considered the budget as a unified whole."[19] Because the congressional budget resolution was the formal vehicle of fiscal policy, the President's actions – limited to signing or vetoing spending and tax bills – became piecemeal. Nevertheless, the President's budget still came first in the process, and was considered the start of budget development (both are still the case today). Most experts refer to the congressional budget as a "response" to the President's, not as the main blueprint for fiscal policy.

The Dominance of Automatic Federal Spending

The problem of automatic government spending traces as far back as the post-Civil War period. For the first 75 years of the republic, both spending and revenue were handled by the House Committee on Ways and Means and the Senate Committee on Finance. After the Civil War, the House and Senate carved out separate Appropriations Committees to handle spending matters. "The arrangement allowed for unified control of spending in one committee. Yet, it did not have authority to control all spending – the size of pensions and other permanent appropriations (together constituting over half the budget) were determined by other committees."[20]

Over the past 50 years, that problem has returned. Most of the Federal Government's automatic spending – formally known as "direct" or "mandatory" spending[21] – flows

---

[17] Matthew C. Spalding, *Congress, Budget Control, and Constitutional Self-Government*, testimony to the Committee on the Budget, U.S. House of Representatives, 25 May 2016. President Roosevelt moved the Bureau of the Budget in his 1939 government reorganization plan.
[18] Schick, op. cit., p. 17.
[19] Philip G. Joyce, testimony to the Committee on the Budget, U.S. House of Representatives, on "Reclaiming Congressional Authority through the Power of the Purse," 25 May 2016.
[20] Wildavsky, op. cit., p. 30.
[21] Section 250 of the Balanced Budget and Emergency Deficit Control Act of 1985 defines "direct spending" as "(A) budget authority provided by law other than appropriations Acts; (B) entitlement authority; and (C) the Supplemental Nutrition Assistance Program."

from effectively permanent authorizations. Programs funded this way – mainly entitlements – pay benefits directly to groups and individuals without an intervening appropriation. They spend without limit. Their totals are determined by numerous factors outside the control of Congress: caseloads, the growth or contraction of GDP, inflation, and many others. To put it simply, spending in these programs is uncontrolled and uncontrollable – because it is designed to be.

In 1965, at the dawn of President Johnson's Great Society, Washington's automatic spending, including interest payments (a mandatory payment in the true sense of the word), represented about 34 percent of the budget. By 1974, when the Congressional Budget Act was adopted, it had swollen to nearly 49 percent of total spending. Today, automatic spending including interest has surged to more than two-thirds of the budget,[22] and in just 10 years it will swell to 78 percent (see Figure 1 below).[23] Automatic spending is the sole source of Federal spending growth as a share of the economy and the main driver of government debt.

Figure 1

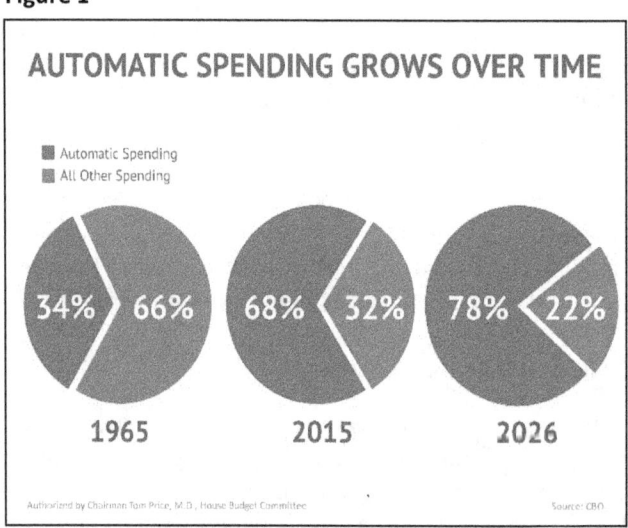

Control of spending, properly understood, means the power to spend *or not to spend* taxpayer money. Automatic/mandatory spending destroys Congress's ability *not* to spend. By design, automatic spending requires a Presidential signature to turn off – the very opposite of the constitutional provision that spending can occur only pursuant to positive legislation appropriating funds. As reflected by Judge Collyer's ruling described earlier, it should be Congress, not the President, deciding whether or not money is spent. Unless Congress can muster a two-thirds supermajority vote to overrule the President, automatic spending will continue on its current path, moving the Nation ever closer to a debt crisis, and Congress is powerless to stop it, notwithstanding its Article I constitutional authority to control spending. With two-thirds of the budget no longer in the control of Congress, the so-called "power of the purse" has been effectively ceded to the Executive Branch.

---

[22] Congressional Budget Office, op. cit., Table 1.
[23] Ibid., Table 1.

Abandoning the 'Regular Order'

On numerous occasions, Congress has failed to adopt budget resolutions or to pass all its appropriations separately or on time (see Figure 2 below). This resulted in continuing resolutions [CRs] of varying magnitudes and amounts, lasting well after the start of the fiscal year, and sometimes late in the calendar year, just as Members are leaving Washington D.C. for the Christmas and New Year's holidays. Sometimes these lapses of appropriations – coupled with impasses between Congress and the White House – have resulted in temporarily shutting down agencies and activities considered non-essential for health, safety, or national security.

Figure 2

THE STATUS QUO IS NOT WORKING

Time Period	Budget Conference Agreements	Appropriations Completed On Time
Past 5 Years	1	0 out of 60
Past 10 Years	4	5 out of 120
Past 25 Years	16	51 out of 314

Authorized by Chairman Tom Price, M.D. House Budget Committee. Source: House Budget Committee

Although lawmakers themselves are ultimately responsible, the current process allows them to postpone politically sensitive bills until a late-year or post-election rush, with no immediately apparent consequences. Furthermore, the process lacks incentives to ensure timely consideration of regular appropriations, leading to increasingly frequent use of omnibus spending bills.

This breakdown of the "regular order" diminishes Congress's policymaking authority in several ways.

- First, the simple inability of Congress to follow its own budget procedures is a *de facto* failure to exercise its governing authority.

- Second, in recent years, the total discretionary spending amounts have been decided not through the budget or appropriations, but in *ad hoc*, short-term budget agreements negotiated among a few members of Congress and the administration. This cedes to the Executive Branch partial authority to determine aggregate spending levels – a decision that, under the Congressional Budget Act, belongs solely to Congress. These budget agreements are mostly done behind closed doors without input from the majority of Congress.

- Third, adopting huge omnibus spending bills means Members are forced to take a single vote up or down on a trillion-dollar package. They cannot differentiate their votes on individual preferences; it is a take-it-or-leave-it proposition for the entire discretionary budget.

- Fourth, such legislation may contain important policy choices heavily influenced by the administration. This was the case with the Bipartisan Budget Act of 2013 – which followed a two-week partial shutdown of government activities in October – and the Bipartisan Budget Act of 2015. In these measures, the administration demanded that every increase in defense discretionary spending had to be matched dollar-for-dollar by increases in non-defense discretionary spending, and Congress accepted.

These budgeting failures also corrode Congress's authority in the eyes of the public. "I have no specific evidence concerning precisely how all of the recent talk about government shutdowns, 'fiscal cliffs,' and late budgets has translated into a specific loss of public faith in the Congress. But it can't have helped. If the Congress is viewed only as a source of gridlock, it not only invites unilateral executive action, but reinforces the notion that the President can get things done and the Congress cannot. I would therefore conclude that timely adherence to the budget timetable not only makes the government work better and cost less, it also strengthens the Congress as an institution."[24]

User Fees and Collections

According to the Office of Management and Budget, the Federal Government collected $516 billion in user fees in 2015. A user fee typically reflects optional business-like transactions between private parties and the government rather than compulsory taxes. These fees, which are booked as offsets to spending rather than as revenue, arguably mask the true size and scope of government activity.

Equally important, many of these fees are available to agencies to spend without further appropriation, which weakens congressional oversight and accountability. In some cases, they prevent Congress from influencing agency behavior because the agencies can essentially operate through fee collections, without appropriations. In other cases, such as in the Asset Forfeiture Fund, user fees are seen as fostering incentives for potential abuse, because the more assets an agency seizes, the larger its budget becomes.

RESTORING CONSTITUTIONAL GOVERNMENT

Piecemeal, incremental fixes to the current budget process will no longer suffice to restore the practice of congressional budgeting. A complete rewrite of the Congressional Budget Act is needed, built on the following principles: exercising constitutional government by reinforcing Congress's power of the purse; promoting and sustaining fiscal responsibility; restoring congressional control of spending and taxing; improving oversight and facilitating orderly decision-making; and reflecting the true costs of government programs.

---

[24] Joyce, op. cit.

For Congress to reclaim its full authority under Article I of the Constitution, this rewrite of the Budget Act must reach deeper than practical or mechanical elements. It should aim not just at fixing current problems in the budget process – of which there are many – but at actually enhancing constitutional government. Among the considerations that can help guide the process are the following:

Figure 3

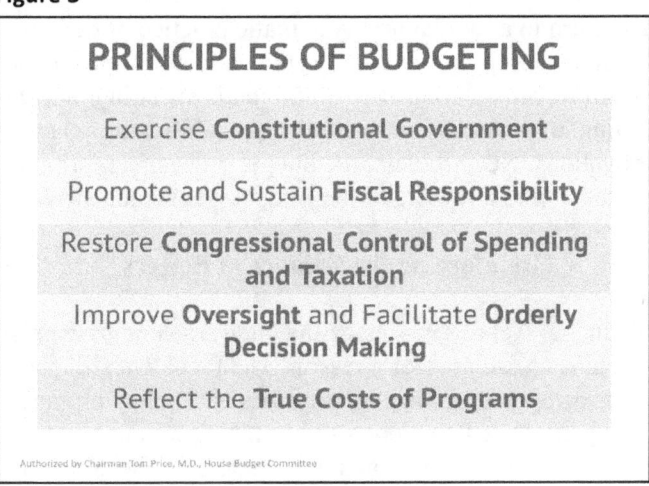

Limiting Government

The principle of limited government runs throughout the Constitution, but is clearly stated in the Tenth Amendment: "The powers not delegated to the United States by the Constitution, nor prohibited by it to the States, are reserved to the States respectively, or to the people." In other words, the Federal Government may not expand beyond the powers expressly defined in the Constitution.

The most readily available means of implementing this principle is the control of spending. If the Constitution was intended to provide a framework for a limited government, a practice of budgeting aimed at limiting spending is one of the best ways to achieve it. Spending is how government does what it does, the reason government taxes and borrows. Hence, spending is the root cause of every other fiscal consequence. Total spending also is one of the best measures of the size and scope of government and its burden on the economy.[25]

Controlling spending is therefore a principal means of limiting government and should be a focus of the budget process. To limit spending is to limit government itself and to validate the principle that "budgeting is governing."

Enhancing Congress's Policymaking Role

Budgeting should be viewed as more than a mechanical or accounting process. It should strengthen Congress's constitutional role as the policymaking institution of the Federal

---

[25] See Douglas J. Holtz-Eakin, testimony in hearing, *Economic Effects of Long-Term Federal Obligations*, Committee on the Budget, U.S. House of Representatives, 24 July 2003.

Government. Therefore, the budget resolution – the only legislative vehicle that views the government comprehensively – should define the priorities guiding its allocation of resources. It should reflect the delegation of powers between the Federal and State governments as envisioned in the Constitution. Embracing these principles gives meaning to the budget resolution as an instrument for governing, and provides coherence to the spending and tax bills that follow.

Congress also must return to a regular and systematic practice of budgeting. This should include passing separate appropriations bills, as the budget process intends, and developing methods of regaining control over automatic spending programs. The best incentive for budgeting, of course, is simply a firm commitment by lawmakers to fulfill their legislative obligations. Nevertheless, the budget process can provide incentives to support that commitment, and a rewrite of the Budget Act should strive to create them.

Reinforcing the Balance of Powers

The Congressional Budget Act of 1974 made the budget a *concurrent* resolution – not requiring the President's signature – for a reason. The President still prepares his budget – an expression of his own agenda, his own priorities and policy proposals – independently of Congress. The President also has the important budgeting role of either signing or vetoing the spending and tax bills that implement the congressional budget. Through veto messages, he can encourage, but not compel, changes in those measures.

When Congress fails to conduct its own regular budget procedures, it cedes to the administration more control over budgetary decisions through its execution of spending and tax policies. This is especially true with entitlements and their effectively permanent authorizations. Because they are not subject to regular congressional review, this major part of the budget is controlled by the administration and its regulatory apparatus.

The United States Government is not a parliamentary system, and its budgeting procedures – so central to governing – should not be designed that way. The budget process should reinforce the Constitution's arrangement of three separate, coequal branches of government by separating powers, not combining them. Preventing a concentration of power in any one branch is essential to preventing the emergence of an autocratic government. The congressional budget should assertively define the allocation of resources in a way that aligns with Congress's vision of national priorities. Congress also should periodically review all spending programs, including entitlements.

Controlling the Administrative State

The vast expansion of the Executive Branch has led to an ever-growing role of government in American society – through regulation rather than legislation (see Figure 4 below). The Progressive impulses that promoted this trend relied largely on policy "experts," shielded from political influence.

In their regulatory capacities, these bureaucrats have come to assume authorities of all three branches of government: legislative, executive, and judicial. Thus, America's constitutional government has increasingly become an administrative state largely run by unelected career government employees. "In fact, the vast majority of 'laws' governing the United States are not passed by Congress but are issued as regulations, crafted largely by thousands of unnamed, unreachable bureaucrats."[26]

"Whether the regulatory agencies are 'executive agencies,' 'executive departments,' 'federal departments,' or 'independent regulatory commissions' is irrelevant. In whatever form they may take, the myriad agencies and departments that make up this administrative state operate as a 'fourth branch' of government that typically combines the powers of the other three and makes policy with little regard for the rights and opinions of citizens."[27]

Figure 4

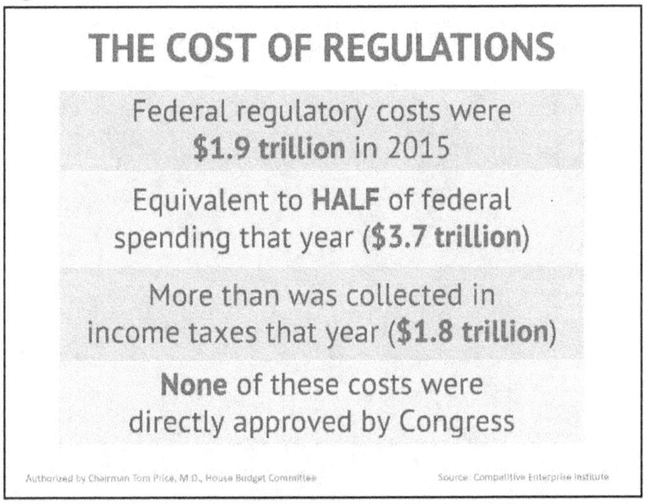

THE COST OF REGULATIONS

Federal regulatory costs were **$1.9 trillion** in 2015

Equivalent to **HALF** of federal spending that year (**$3.7 trillion**)

More than was collected in income taxes that year (**$1.8 trillion**)

None of these costs were directly approved by Congress

Authorized by Chairman Tom Price, M.D., House Budget Committee — *Source: Competitive Enterprise Institute*

In addition to taking firmer control of the regulatory process itself, Congress could address this problem through budgeting. "Reversing the trend of a diminishing legislature and the continued expansion of the executive falls largely to Congress, which must rebuild itself to control the operations of government, break the administrative state, and provide a robust check on the modern executive. . . . This will be a battle that must be fought on many fronts, but a crucial piece of that effort will be reviving the power of the purse as a tool to help return lawmaking powers to Congress and restore fiscal responsibility."[28]

CONCLUSION

No single activity consumes as much of Congress's time as budgeting – choosing priorities and allocating financial resources accordingly. These are among the most fundamental ways for a legislature to shape governing policies. Moreover, the budget process amounts to a direct exercise of the form of government a country has. In the

---

[26] Jonathan Turley, "The Rise of the Fourth Branch," *The Washington Post*, 26 May 2013, http://articles.washingtonpost.com/2013-05-24/opinions/39495251_1_federal-agencies-federal-government-fourth-branch.
[27] Joseph Postell, *From Administrative State to Constitutional Government*, Heritage Foundation Special Report No. 116, 7 December 2012. p. 5: http://www.heritage.org/research/reports/2012/12/from-administrative-state-to-constitutional-government.
[28] Spalding, op. cit.

United States, the budget system is essential to maintaining the Federal Government's arrangement of three separate but coequal branches. The budget process must reinforce basic constitutional principles.

The Founders granted Congress the principal role in formulating national policy, and created a separate, independent Executive Branch to execute it. It is not a parliamentary structure; it consists of three coequal branches, each with distinct powers. The budget process should not merely accommodate the constitutional system, but should actively strive to enhance it. Strengthening Congress's Article I authority should be a central consideration of budget process reform.

CONTRIBUTERS

This working paper was prepared by the following members of the House Budget Committee majority staff:

Jim Bates, Chief Counsel
Jim Herz, Policy Director and Director of Budget Review
Mary Popadiuk, Counsel
Jenna Spealman, Policy Advisor
Patrick Louis Knudsen, Associate Policy Advisor

All can be reached at:

Committee on the Budget
U.S. House of Representatives
207 Cannon House Office Building
202-226-7270

www.ingramcontent.com/pod-product-compliance
Lightning Source LLC
Chambersburg PA
CBHW080535190526
45169CB00008B/3184